GARR

D0426595

Bristlecone pines are the oldest trees in the world.

Hard, spiky leaves keep insects away.

New needles

Crab apples growing in the wild

The tough, needle-like leaves of the Norway spruce can stay on the tree all year long.

Very few seedlings can grow into trees.

Mass of beech seedlings coming up together

Pig searching for tasty beech nuts under a tree

EXPLORERS

Trees

Written by
LINDA GAMLIN

DORLING KINDERSLEY, INC.

NEW YORK

A DORLING KINDERSLEY BOOK

Editor Jodi Block **Art editors** Thomas Keenes, Susan Downing
Senior editor Susan McKeever **Assistant editor** Djinn von Noorden
U.S. editor Charles A. Wills
Production Catherine Semark **Photography by** Roger Phillips
Editorial consultant Theresa Greenaway

First American Edition, 1993
4 6 8 10 9 7 5 3
Published in the United States by
Dorling Kindersley, Inc., 95 Madison Avenue
New York, New York 10016
Copyright © 1993
Dorling Kindersley Limited, London
Text copyright © 1993 Linda Gamlin

ISBN 1-56458-230-2

Library of Congress Catalog Card Number 92-54310

Color reproduction by Colourscan, Singapore
Printed in Italy by A. Mondadori Editore, Verona

Contents

Looking at trees

If you were describing a friend, you might talk about their hair, eyes, clothes, and height. To describe a tree, you need to get to know it in the same sort of detail – the leaves, flowers, twigs, and bark. Look at growth patterns, too. Which way do the branches point, and where are the longest ones?

Family tree
Looking closely at a tree may tell you something about its nearest relatives. The flowers of the laburnum tree are just like those of peas and beans, showing that they all belong to the same plant family.

A laburnum leaf is made up of three leaflets, like a clover.

In spring, look for long chains of yellow flowers hanging from the tree.

🖐 *Laburnum pods have poisonous black seeds – so don't eat them!*

Shaping up
Trees come in many different shapes. The wind and the amount of sunlight change a tree's shape, but the basic growth pattern stays the same. Can you find a tree to fit each of these shapes?

Round shape: beech

Upswept branches – fastigiate hornbeam (left), Lombardy poplar (right)

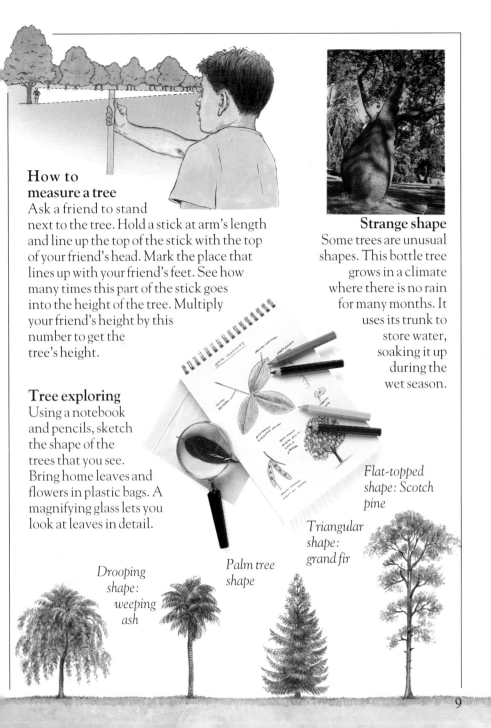

How to measure a tree

Ask a friend to stand next to the tree. Hold a stick at arm's length and line up the top of the stick with the top of your friend's head. Mark the place that lines up with your friend's feet. See how many times this part of the stick goes into the height of the tree. Multiply your friend's height by this number to get the tree's height.

Tree exploring

Using a notebook and pencils, sketch the shape of the trees that you see. Bring home leaves and flowers in plastic bags. A magnifying glass lets you look at leaves in detail.

Strange shape

Some trees are unusual shapes. This bottle tree grows in a climate where there is no rain for many months. It uses its trunk to store water, soaking it up during the wet season.

Flat-topped shape: Scotch pine

Triangular shape: grand fir

Drooping shape: weeping ash

Palm tree shape

What is a tree?

A tree is just a plant on stilts. Or on one stilt, to be exact. That stilt is called a trunk, and its job is to get the leaves as high in the air as possible. Plants feed on sunlight and being tall is a way to get more light. Being tall also keeps tree leaves out of reach of hungry animals such as deer and goats.

An oak tree is a broadleaf. The leaves are thin and flat.

Paper leaves or needle leaves?

There are two main types of tree – conifers and broadleaves. You can tell them apart by their leaves. Conifers (below) have leaves like needles, or like tiny scales. Broadleaves (right) all have leaves that are thin and flat, as if they were cut out of green paper.

This bunya pine is a conifer and has needle-like leaves.

Rounded or triangular?

You can usually tell whether a tree is a conifer or a broadleaf by looking at its shape. Broad-leaved trees are usually rounded. Conifers (left) tend to grow into a triangular shape. The giant tree on the opposite page looks like an upside-down carrot.

Fighting for light

A forest may seem peaceful, but there is a silent battle going on – a battle for light. Each tree is trying to grow taller and spread itself wider, so that it can get more light than its neighbors.

Living fossils

Ginkgos are odd trees – neither conifers nor broadleaves. All their close relatives died out millions of years ago. Despite the shape of their leaves, they are most closely related to conifers.

Ginkgo leaves are fan-shaped and divided in two.

Palm impersonators

Tree ferns are just giant ferns. They flourished long ago, but now there are only a few survivors left. Cycads are ancient cousins of the conifers. Both look like palm trees, but this is just coincidence – they are not related.

Tree test

Is it really a tree? To make the grade it must be over twenty feet tall and have only one main stem – called a trunk. Anything else is a shrub. A young tree that has yet to reach twenty feet is called a sapling.

Tall trees

Redwoods are the tallest trees in the world. They grow more than 360 feet high. That makes even a giraffe look tiny!

11

Parts of a tree

A tree is made up of many parts, all working together to make it grow. The leaves make food using sunlight and gases in the air. The roots take water and minerals from the soil. The leaves need water to do their job, and the roots need food to help them grow. So the tree trunk acts as a highway, with water rushing up, and sap (food) rushing down.

Hollow tree

A tree's water and sap channels lie just underneath the outermost layer of bark, so the center of a trunk is not vital to its survival. This tree has split completely in two but is still alive.

Moving parts

By cutting off a bud from one tree and grafting (transplanting) it onto the trunk of another, people can create very unusual trees. The tree shown here is a laburnum (yellow flowers) with just one grafted branch from a Judas tree (pink flowers).

Thirsty leaves

See for yourself how a leafy twig sucks up water. Find two twigs and put them into glass jars. Remove the leaves from one of them. Add exactly the same amount of water to both jars and mark the level. Very carefully, pour a layer of oil onto the water. After a week check the water levels. How do they compare?

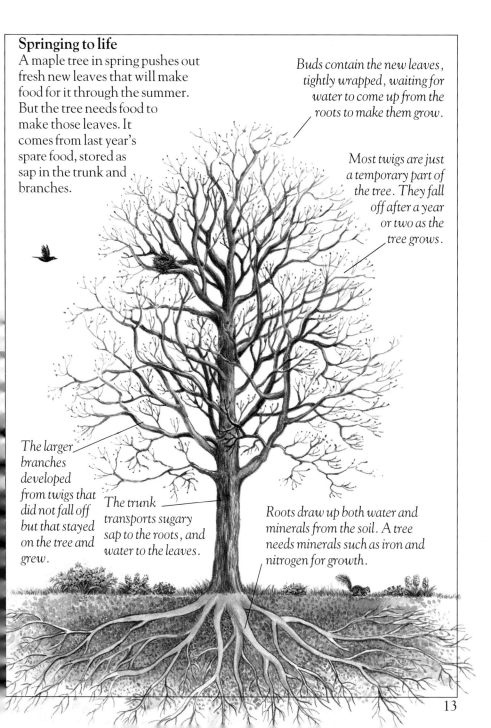

Springing to life

A maple tree in spring pushes out
fresh new leaves that will make
food for it through the summer.
But the tree needs food to
make those leaves. It
comes from last year's
spare food, stored as
sap in the trunk and
branches.

*Buds contain the new leaves,
tightly wrapped, waiting for
water to come up from the
roots to make them grow.*

*Most twigs are just
a temporary part of
the tree. They fall
off after a year
or two as the
tree grows.*

*The larger
branches
developed
from twigs that
did not fall off
but that stayed
on the tree and
grew.*

*The trunk
transports sugary
sap to the roots, and
water to the leaves.*

*Roots draw up both water and
minerals from the soil. A tree
needs minerals such as iron and
nitrogen for growth.*

13

Bark – the skin of a tree

In the trunk of a tree there are tiny pipes that carry water up from the soil and sugary sap down from the leaves to the roots. Bark protects these delicate pipes. As a tree grows, the trunk gets too fat for its coat of bark, which cracks open on the outside. But there is always new bark growing underneath to replace it.

Syrup from sap

Maple syrup comes from the sugar maple, a North American tree. People cut small holes into the pipes in the trunk and collect the sap that drips out. Then they boil the sap to remove most of the water, leaving maple syrup.

The white bark of a silver birch often has black diamond shapes.

Thin skin

Silver birch has very thin bark that peels off in strips as the tree grows. The lines on the bark are rows of breathing pores, called lenticels. These take in oxygen from the air so the tree can breathe.

Boats from bark

Birch trees have unusually thin and flexible bark. Some tribes of North American Indians once used it for building canoes and making shelters.

Bark patterns

When the old bark of a tree cracks and breaks, it forms interesting patterns. You can record these patterns by "bark rubbing." Attach some strong paper to the tree trunk with clear tape. Rub firmly over the paper with a wax crayon. Label the rubbing to show what type of tree it came from. Do the patterns vary with the type of tree?

A young tree has thin, smooth bark, but bark thickens with age.

Resin to the rescue

Resin oozes from pine trees when the trunk is damaged. This keeps wood-eating insects out, and kills bacteria and fungi that could infect the wounded tree.

Scaly bark

Most bark slowly cracks into pieces and eventually falls from its tree. But the bark of plane trees falls off regularly in flat scales, revealing fresh bark. The scales take away all the dirt and soot on the trunk, so plane trees can survive in polluted cities.

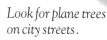

Look for plane trees on city streets.

Dirt clogs the breathing pores on bark, but plane trees throw it off.

15

Green for life

If you were a plant, you would never need to eat, because you could make all the food you needed inside your own body. Just sunbathe for awhile – you need the sun to make food – and you would feel well fed. The bad news is that you would be green! The pigment (coloring) that can take the energy from sunlight and turn it into food is green. It is known as chlorophyll (*klor-oh-fill*.)

The saguaro's stems store water and act as leaves, making food with the help of the sun.

Tree with no leaves
The saguaro cactus is a type of tree. But, like other cacti, it has no leaves. The saguaro can still survive because the chlorophyll is there in its green stems, working hard to trap the sun's energy and turn it into food.

Where's the green gone?
Even though these copper beech leaves look purple, they still contain chlorophyll. Purple pigments hide the green color, but the chlorophyll is there underneath.

Invisible plumbing

A magnolia leaf looks glossy and smooth. But as a fallen leaf rots away, you can see the network of veins inside. These carry water to every part of the leaf and take away the food the leaf has produced.

The more the leaf rots, the more you can see its tiny veins.

Watching leaves breathe

Leaves are breathing all the time. They take some gases in and give others out. As this happens they automatically lose water vapor from their leaves.

Secure the bag to make it airtight.

1 You cannot see water vapor – it is just a gas. This is what comes out of the leaves, in a process called evaporation. If you put a plastic bag over the leaves, you can make the water vapor turn back into water.

2 Check your leaves every hour. Can you see water droplets inside the bag? When water vapor changes back into water, this is called condensation.

Prickles keep deer away, while chemicals in the leaves ward off insects.

Keeping green

Most broad-leaved trees lose their leaves in winter, but a holly is an evergreen broad-leaved tree. To succeed as an evergreen, it needs tough leaves to keep moisture in and animals away.

Broadleaves

The leaves of broad-leaved trees come in a thousand different shapes and sizes. They are called broadleaves because their leaves are thin, flat, and often wide. If you live in Europe or North America, you'll find that most broadleaves are deciduous – they drop their leaves for the winter. In most other parts of the world, broadleaves are evergreen.

The pattern of the veins can help you identify a tree.

Veins carry food and water around the leaf.

Norway maple leaf

Broader leaves
The Norway maple is a broadleaf whose leaves are sometimes broader than they are long. Most maples have hand-shaped leaves – stretch your fingers as wide as you can to see the basic shape.

Norway maple tree

Striped snake

Not all maple leaves are hand-shaped. This snakebark maple leaf is shaped more like an arrowhead. Snakebark maples have striped bark – now can you guess how they got their name?

This snakebark leaf has jagged edges and a pointed tip.

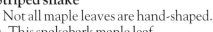

Lots of leaves

At the end of every summer, many broad-leaved trees drop their leaves. On a large maple tree, at least half a million leaves can come tumbling down to the ground – enough to make a heap five feet high. That's taller than you!

Rub a leaf

You can make a record of vein patterns by laying a broadleaf upside down and putting paper over it. Rub the paper gently with a soft pencil and see the pattern appear. Remember to label your leaf rubbing when you have finished.

Sumac leaves are red when they first appear in spring.

Leaves within leaves

Some leaves look as if they have been cut into smaller leaflets with a pair of scissors. The sumac (*soo-mac*) has leaves like this, called compound leaves. Look for wild sumacs in North America or planted ones in gardens all over the world.

Spiky leaves

Conifers such as pines and spruces are the toughest trees you'll find. Their leaves are hard, spiky needles that keep hungry visitors at bay. Deer, caterpillars, and other leaf-eating animals generally cannot eat these needles. Most other conifers are just as well protected with bad-tasting leathery leaves or scales.

Everlasting leaves

Because they are tough and not easily damaged by frost, conifer needles can stay on the tree all winter. The trees, which often live in barren places, save energy by not making a new set of leaves each year. Each needle stays on the tree for three to four years.

Norway spruce leaves are too tough for most insects to eat.

New needles are light green and prickly.

Christmas tree

You might look forward to a Christmas tree in December. Christmas trees are often firs, pines, or spruces. If your tree has roots, you can plant it in a large tub or bucket after the holiday.

Smell and taste

If you've ever taken a walk through a redwood forest you know how nice it smells. But the lovely aroma of coast redwood trees comes from foul-tasting chemicals in their leaves. An insect that chews into them soon gets a nasty taste in its mouth.

Redwood leaves are strap-shaped and leathery.

Each of these tiny scales is a single leaf.

Saving water

Wellingtonia, also called giant sequoia, is a relative of the redwood, but its leaves are very different. The tiny scale-like leaves fit tightly to the stem, helping the tree reduce water loss. Other conifers such as cypresses have the same sort of leaves.

Dinosaur dinner

For some dinosaurs, conifer leaves were edible – if not exactly delicious. Large lumbering plant-eaters such as hadrosaurs had hard bony beaks to tear off and crush the leaves. Chances are they also had indigestion after their meal, but we'll never know!

21

Twigs and buds

Twigs stick out from trees like thousands of tiny fingers. They are the growing end of the tree. Each twig has some buds which contain new shoots. When the time is right, these buds open. The shoots lengthen and then become new twigs. Buds also contain new leaves and flowers.

At the heart of the horse chestnut bud is the young flower, and around it the young leaves.

Sticky scales protect the bud from hungry insects by gumming up their mouths.

Next year's leaves and flowers are all packed tightly inside the buds.

Bud scales from last year left these "girdle scars."

One of last year's leaves left this large smiling scar when it fell.

Smiling twigs
Horse chestnuts have unusually large buds and leaves. When these fall, they leave scars on the twigs that are unique to the horse chestnut. Look for leaf scars that are shaped like big smiling mouths. They have a row of dots where veins ran from the twig into the leaf.

Horse chestnut tree

Just add water!

Leaves and flowers are packed tightly inside a bud, much like dried vegetables or dried soup in a packet. All they need to make them expand is water – as you can prove for yourself!

1 Carefully cut two or three long twigs from a horse chestnut tree, using pruning shears. Ask permission if the tree is in someone's garden or yard.

2 Keep the twigs in clean water on a windowsill. Measure the leaves everyday and see how fast they expand. Make drawings of them, too.

Rising from the flames

Eucalyptus trees grow mostly in dry forests, where fires occur naturally. Even after a fire, the buds of some eucalyptus trees start to grow. They have thick, fire-resistant bark, which protects the buds underneath it, so the tree springs back to life.

Thorny problems

Young leaves are delicious to animals such as deer, goats, and antelopes. Some trees

Thorns are different shapes and can help to identify the tree. This is a false acacia.

have developed thorns to keep these leaf-eaters away. Even if the tree is in a city park, far from its original enemies, it still has thorns.

23

Blossoms

Have you ever wondered why trees have such beautiful blossoms? They need colorful, sweet-smelling flowers to attract bees or other insects. When these animals visit the flowers and drink their nectar, they also transfer pollen from male flowers to female flowers. Once this happens, female flowers make seeds that may grow into new trees.

Budding bark
Not all flowers sprout from twigs. Some of the smaller rain forest trees have flowers on their trunks. Before the petals can open out, the bud has to grow right through the bark.

As birds mop up nectar with the tips of their tongues, they carry pollen from flower to flower.

Stamen

There are about 500 different kinds of eucalyptus trees.

Flowers without petals
Eucalyptus flowers do not have petals. They have masses of cream, white, or red stamens – the part of the flower that contains pollen. These make the flowers look like little brushes. Nectar is hidden at the base of these stamens.

Using its front legs, the honeybee combs pollen into pollen baskets on its hind legs.

Apple flowers have flat, open petals that make it easy for bees to gather pollen and nectar.

Busy bees

You'll see lots of honey bees buzzing around apple blossom. They fly from flower to flower, drinking nectar and spreading pollen. They also store pollen and nectar and bring it back to their hives – where they make honey.

From flower to fruit

Without the help of insects, apple blossom would never become apples. You can do a simple experiment to prove this. Cover a few unopened buds with a fine net bag and tie it securely. This will stop insects from visiting the flowers. Unlike the flowers left uncovered, those inside the bag do not turn into apples.

Watch for hoverflies darting around these flowers – they like to feed on the nectar.

🖐 Make sure you have permission before covering any blossoms.

Reaching for nectar

A horsechestnut blossom has nectar at the bottom of a flower tube. Only an insect with a long proboscis (tongue) can reach in far enough to drink it.

Catkins

If each of the flowers in a catkin were the size of a rose, it would be the biggest bunch of flowers you had ever seen. A catkin is a sausage-shaped cluster of tiny flowers. Catkins rely mostly on wind, but sometimes on insects, to carry pollen from the male flowers. Some reaches the female flowers, which then grow into fruits.

Nectar is produced deep down in the male flowers, at the center of the catkin.

Male catkins are gray at first and turn yellow when the pollen is ripe.

Each female flower has a yellow stigma that collects pollen.

Furry flowers

Pussy willow gets its name from its catkins, because they are plump and furry like kittens. Most catkins hang down so the wind can easily spread their pollen, but not these. Instead they attract bees by producing nectar, and the bees transfer the pollen to female flowers.

White for flight

Each female pussy willow flower turns into a fruit. These fruits are green, but when ripe they split open to release masses of white, fluffy seeds. Look for these woolly seeds blowing off the trees in the early summer.

Each seed of the pussy willow fruit has a fluffy tail so that it can float away on the breeze.

Pussy willow tree

Lambs' tails
Long catkins, such as hazels, are sometimes called lambs' tails, because they look like little tails hanging from the trees.

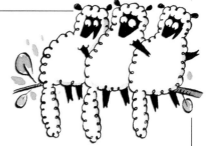

The wind makes the catkin dance around, shaking out its pollen.

Male and female
On some trees, male and female catkins look the same. But on a hazel they look very different. Only the male is a typical catkin. The female catkin looks like a tiny vase with bright pink bristles at the top.

Pollen floating in the air sticks to the bristles of the female flowers.

Millions of pollen grains blow from the male catkins.

After pollination, female flowers will become a cluster of hazel nuts.

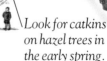

Look for catkins on hazel trees in the early spring.

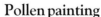

Pollen painting
Hazels flower in early spring, when there is usually plenty of wind for pollination. But you can lend a hand. Collect pollen on a dry paint-brush and dust it onto the female flowers.

Woody cones

You can find cones on coniferous trees, such as pines and firs. They do the same job as flowers do on other trees. Male cones produce pollen, which is blown to female cones by the wind. When the pollen lands on female cones, seeds begin to grow. The cone scales harden and close to protect the seeds.

Young Douglas fir cones

Young and green
When young cones develop they are quite soft and flexible – they only become woody later. Young Douglas fir cones are green and always hang downward from the tree.

Douglas fir tree

Scale

Seed

Douglas fir cones fall to the ground intact, so they are easy to collect.

Growing old
Young Douglas fir cones usually ripen in one season. The male cones wither and fall once their pollen is gone. But the female cones get larger and fatter as the seeds swell up inside them. This Douglas fir cone has been cut in half so you can see where it stores the seeds.

Free fall
Seeds fall from cones in order to grow into new trees. If seeds fall beneath the parent tree they will not have enough light to grow. Conifer seeds have a papery wing attached to them, which acts like a little propeller. They spin and blow in the wind, far away from the parent tree.

Flying Douglas fir seeds

Cone colors

Young female larch cones are bright red and look a bit like flowers. After pollination they turn green and start to expand – until they become hard, brown cones. Old cones stay on the tree long after the seeds have fallen, sometimes for many years.

Mature cone

Young cone

Open sesame

It would be a mistake for seeds to fall on a rainy day, because they would not be able to blow around on the breeze. So cones only open when it is warm and dry. Try putting a closed cone near a radiator to see what happens.

You will not find cedar cones on the ground – they break up while still on the tree.

Smooth scales

Cedar cones are egg-shaped and almost completely smooth, because the scales overlap so tightly. The seeds take two years to ripen, and then the cones open.

29

Tasty fruits and nuts

Not all trees rely on wind to carry their seeds away from the parent tree. Some trees use their fruits to persuade animals to spread their seeds. Some fruits have a tasty pulp with small seeds that are left behind in the animal's droppings. Others have a tasty seed, or nut, many of which are eaten or stored by animals. But some are forgotten and grow into trees.

Where's lunch?
Squirrels bury nuts, then dig them up in winter, when food is short. They never find all the nuts. Some survive and are ready to grow when spring arrives.

This coconut was washed up here by the sea.

The white "flesh" is food for the young tree.

Thick fibrous "matting" keeps the coconut afloat on the sea.

The shell is waterproof.

Putting down roots
A coconut has enough of its own water inside the shell to keep the young tree alive until its roots are well developed.

Coconut capsule
A coconut is like a spaceship: a sealed capsule that can ensure survival in a totally alien environment. The thick shell keeps out salty seawater that spells death to a land plant.

Red delicious

Granny Smith

Cultivated apple tree

Crab apple tree

Wild apples
The fruit we eat has changed a lot from wild fruit. The ancestors of modern apples were tiny, sour crab apples. For thousands of years, farmers have cultivated trees with larger, sweeter fruit, so we can eat delicious apples.

The seeds turn from white to brown as the apple ripens.

Bitter sweet
You might find wild crab apples in woods and hedges, but don't eat them! They taste very bitter to us, but animals love them. Crows and deer help these trees by scattering their seeds. Cultivated apples do not need animals because people grow the trees.

Sweet and juicy
Wild crab apple trees and old-fashioned, cultivated apple trees were about the same size. But the cultivated apple trees that we see today are very low-growing – so the apples are easy to pick.

Making fruit prints
Using firm fruits, you can make prints in different colors and use them to decorate cards or wrapping paper. Carefully cut apples and pears lengthwise, and oranges across the middle. Mix up poster paints in a pie plate, dip the fruit in, and press lightly on the paper. Do you see where the fruit stored its seeds?

31

Getting out of the seed

Packed inside each seed is a tiny tree waiting to be born. A special store of food gives the seed enough energy to stay alive until it is ready to germinate (begin growing). Some seeds have a small supply of food and must germinate a few days after leaving the tree. Others, such as beech seeds, can survive months of cold weather before they begin to grow.

Beech tree

Prickly case hides two nuts

Ripe nuts have tough glossy skin

Prickly problem

Beech trees produce thousands of beech nuts every autumn. The tender young nuts grow inside hard, prickly cases that keep out the insects that would otherwise feed on them. By the time the cases open up and the nuts fall out, they have their own hard brown skin to protect them.

Beech feast

Many of the beech nuts that fall from the tree do not survive the cold winter months. Hungry animals, such as wild boar and pigs, eat the oil-rich beech seeds without helping to scatter them.

Planting a tree

Try growing a beech seed. Collect beech nuts when they fall and keep them outside in a pot of damp sand. They need many months of cold weather to germinate.

1 In the spring, soak the seeds overnight in warm water before planting them.

2 Plant them in pots of fine soil or potting mix. A plastic bag over the top means that you won't have to water them so often.

3 Keep an eye on the pots and remove the plastic bag when the beech seedling appears. It will need strong light now – either outside, if it is warm enough, or on a sunny windowsill.

Fire lovers

Some eucalyptus seeds develop inside a hard case that needs to be burned by flames before it will break open. The best time for a young eucalyptus to begin life is after a bushfire.

Watching trees grow

Trees need light to grow, plus water and minerals from the soil. If tree seeds sprout in a forest, the taller trees block out most of the light. When a large tree is blown down, light floods through onto the forest floor. Young trees can then grow, and the fastest will shade out the other young trees.

Too close for comfort
Beech trees produce thousands of seeds each year, but only one or two will grow up to be trees. None of the trees shown above is likely to succeed – they are growing too close together.

Baby beech tree
Watch the seed you started to grow on the last page sprout into a beech tree. The seed leaves contain a store of food that keeps the baby tree going until it has its first true leaves. Then it can make food for itself.

True leaves are just like those on the adult tree.

Seed leaves

The seed leaves expand as water comes up from the root.

The stem is growing fast, pushing the leaves up toward the light.

The root is throwing out rootlets to get more water.

The root has pushed out of the seed case.

Eyes everywhere!

If you walk through a beech forest, you may feel that eyes are everywhere! This is because trees drop some branches as they grow, leaving a mark on the trunk that looks like a large, staring eye. Other trees show these marks, but not as clearly as a beech.

Eye on a beech tree

Old father pine

The oldest trees in the world are the bristlecone pines of the Rocky Mountains. Some of these twisted little trees may be 6,000 years old. That makes them some of the oldest living things on Earth.

With enough water and sunlight, the beech tree may be this height in its second year.

This ten-year-old beech tree is much taller than a ten-year-old boy or girl.

Growing up

All trees grow in two directions – upward and outward. Each year the twigs grow longer, while the trunk, branches, and roots grow wider. The roots spread as widely underground as the branches do above ground. A beech tree can continue to grow for 200 years.

A beech tree takes 200 years to get this big. Other kinds of trees might do it in 70 years.

Changing seasons

In some parts of the world, there is a huge difference between the seasons – between summer and winter, or between the dry season and the rainy season. Trees have to adapt to the changing seasons as best they can. Some lose all their leaves in the winter or in the dry season, while others shed just some of their leaves.

Monsoon madness
The monsoon climate – long dry seasons followed by months of heavy rainfall – is tough on trees. They adapt by shedding their leaves in the dry season, and shutting down until the rains return.

Tender young leaves have burst from their buds.

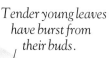

Many insects appear in warm weather and damage summer leaves.

Spring
In spring, a deciduous tree in the northern half of the world produces new leaves. The leaves are curled up inside the buds. They expand quickly, and begin making food for the tree.

Summer
During summer, the leaves grow darker and tougher to keep hungry leaf-eating insects at bay. Some trees grow another set of leaves to replace those that have been eaten.

Small change

Forests near the equator –
such as this rain forest in
northeastern Australia
– have just about the
same climate all year
round. The farther
you travel from
the equator,
the more the
temperatures
change
between
seasons.

*How many colors
can you see on an
autumn tree?*

*Conifers keep their
leaves all winter,
ready for a quick
start in spring.*

*The branches are bare,
but next year's leaves
are hidden in the buds.*

Autumn

Chlorophyll makes leaves green.
Before the leaves fall, the tree breaks
down its chlorophyll so that the leaves
lose their green color. Other chemical
changes may make them red or yellow.

Winter

The tree is inactive until spring,
so no matter how cold and icy
the winter, its leaves cannot be
damaged. They are safely packed
away inside winter buds.

Trees' enemies

Trees have many natural enemies, especially animals that eat the leaves. These can be as small as a caterpillar or as large as a moose. Wood is not as nutritious as leaves, but some insects and fungi use it for food.

To add to these problems, people hurt trees by causing pollution, such as acid rain.

The gases can travel great distances before falling as acid rain.

This bracket fungus eats away at trees, killing many every year.

Rain damage

Exhaust fumes from cars, and smoke from fires, factories, and power stations, all release poisonous gases into the air. When the gases mix with water they fall as acid rain. If the rain is too acid, trees lose their leaves and die.

Deadly fungi

Fungi that feed on wood are among a tree's greatest enemies. The fungi push tiny feeding threads into the wood, which can infect the tree.

Tree stranglers

Tropical strangler figs live up to their name! They wind around the whole tree, smothering its trunk and branches. The tree eventually dies.

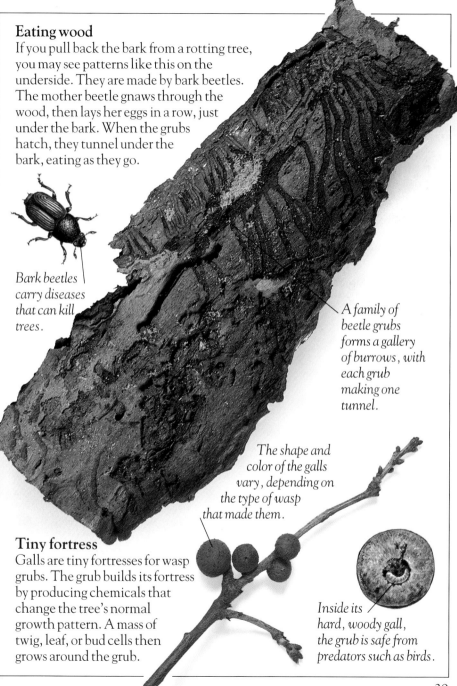

Eating wood

If you pull back the bark from a rotting tree, you may see patterns like this on the underside. They are made by bark beetles. The mother beetle gnaws through the wood, then lays her eggs in a row, just under the bark. When the grubs hatch, they tunnel under the bark, eating as they go.

Bark beetles carry diseases that can kill trees.

A family of beetle grubs forms a gallery of burrows, with each grub making one tunnel.

The shape and color of the galls vary, depending on the type of wasp that made them.

Tiny fortress

Galls are tiny fortresses for wasp grubs. The grub builds its fortress by producing chemicals that change the tree's normal growth pattern. A mass of twig, leaf, or bud cells then grows around the grub.

Inside its hard, woody gall, the grub is safe from predators such as birds.

Trees' friends

A tree is like an apartment building – it is home to hundreds of living things. Some animals and fungi feed on the tree itself. Others live in the tree, and they may help the tree by eating its enemies. This is called "mutualism," because each does the other some good.

Best friends
This chickadee is one of the tree's best friends. It eats many of the caterpillars, aphids, and other insects that like to nibble the tree's leaves or suck its sap.

Guarding ants
Whistling thorn acacia trees have special hollow spaces at the base of their spines where ants can nest. In return for their free home, the ferocious stinging ants keep away leaf-eaters, such as antelopes.

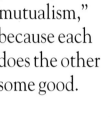

Hug a tree
In the Indian Himalayas, local people have stopped their forests from being cut down by hugging the trees. Try hugging a tree yourself – what does the bark feel like?

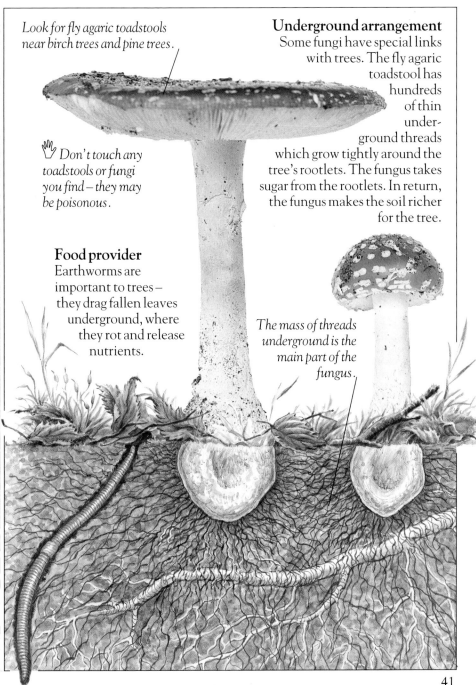

Look for fly agaric toadstools near birch trees and pine trees.

✋ *Don't touch any toadstools or fungi you find – they may be poisonous.*

Underground arrangement
Some fungi have special links with trees. The fly agaric toadstool has hundreds of thin underground threads which grow tightly around the tree's rootlets. The fungus takes sugar from the rootlets. In return, the fungus makes the soil richer for the tree.

Food provider
Earthworms are important to trees – they drag fallen leaves underground, where they rot and release nutrients.

The mass of threads underground is the main part of the fungus.

Hardworking wood

Trees provide us with a very useful gift: wood. The first tools made by the earliest people were probably wooden sticks for digging up edible roots. Three million years later, we still use wood in dozens of different ways – for boats, tables, toys, and more!

Pole carving

North American Indians carved totem poles using a single trunk from a large coniferous tree. The totem pole design tells a story.

Timber!

Cutting down a tree is a tricky job. Lumberjacks specialize in felling (cutting down) trees. But even *they* wear safety helmets, to guard against falling branches.

Felled trees

How old is it?

You can tell how old a tree is by counting its rings after it has been cut down. The pale ring is the spring growth, the narrower, darker ring is the summer growth. Each pair marks one year.

From wood to music

A guitar is traditionally made of wood, and the type of wood used is very important. What matters most is the wood on the upper surface of the body (the soundboard) because this picks up the vibrations of the strings and makes them much louder.

The strings are pressed against the fingerboard, which is often made of ebony.

Ebony is a hard black wood from tropical rain forests.

The back of the guitar need not be made of such good wood as the soundboard.

The neck of the guitar is usually made of mahogany or cedar.

The soundboard may be cut from pine, spruce, or cedar.

Sounds of Spain

Guitar music became very popular with Spanish dancers in the 17th century. Today people play guitar all over the world.

Made of ebony, the bridge sends the string's vibrations to the soundboard.

43

Useful trees

You may already know about some of the things we get from trees – wood, paper, and maple syrup. But did you know we also get rubber and cork? Perhaps the best thing is something we cannot see – oxygen. Every growing tree pumps life-saving oxygen into the air and removes carbon dioxide. Too much carbon dioxide can make the Earth too warm.

Cork from a tree
Cork comes from the bark of the cork oak – a tree that grows around the Mediterranean.

Pop!
Fizzy drinks such as champagne need wires to hold the cork in place. When you release the wires, out pops the cork.

Thick-skinned tree
Cork oak bark is extremely thick, to keep in the tree's moisture. It contracts (gets smaller) if you squeeze it and then expands later. After you squeeze a cork into the neck of a bottle, it expands slightly, which keeps it firmly in place.

Making paper

We make paper from fibers in wood. In factories, tree trunks are minced up into pulp – a mushy kind of substance that is then turned into paper. But paper can also be made from old paper – which is how we recycle it. To do this at home you'll need newspaper, wire netting that an adult has nailed to a frame, a saucepan, and an old blanket.

Make sure the pulp is spread evenly over the netting.

From paper we can make books!

1 Shred a clean newspaper into water. Ask an adult to boil it up in an old saucepan until it turns into a mushy pulp.

2 Dip wire netting into the pulp. Lift it out flat and let it drain. Then turn it out onto a piece of blanket. Add two or three more layers on top of the first layer.

3 Put a piece of blanket on top, then a board. Dance on the board to squeeze the water out. Peel back the blanket and let the paper dry.

Rubber is the gummy sap of a tropical tree – the rubber tree.

Spinning sap

Cyclists race through the streets on tires made of rubber. How many other objects you can find that are made of rubber?

Go with the flow

The sap of rubber trees is collected by tapping – making cuts in the bark and collecting the sticky juice that flows out. This juice can be turned into rubber.

Epiphytes

Some figs throw roots down to the ground.

Tropical rain forest

Unlimited moisture and plenty of sunlight mean that trees can grow and grow – and that's exactly what happens in a tropical rain forest. The trees compete with each other frantically for the light and reach tremendous heights as a result. To help support themselves, some have buttress roots that act like giant props.

Reaching for the sun

In this Australian rain forest, you can see several different ways in which plants reach for the sun. Lianas, epiphytes (*ep-ee-fites*), and some figs hitch a ride on the tallest trees. Tree ferns make do with the dim light lower down in the forest.

Lianas

Can you spot the red-eyed tree frog resting in the tree ferns?

Buttress roots spread out and stop the tree falling over.

Palm leaves are tough and leathery.

Mahogany leaves are compound.

Fan palm

Mahogany tree

Prize wood

True mahogany, from South and Central America, is one of the most beautiful rain forest woods. Because of this, many have been cut down – and now the trees are quite rare.

Fruits of the forest

If you've ever tasted a mango, you'll know how strong its smell is. Mangoes are a rain forest fruit. Their powerful aroma grows stronger as they ripen, to attract animals searching for a meal.

Vanishing forests

Rain forests are being destroyed at an alarming rate, some for timber, others for the land that lies underneath. The land is rarely good enough for farming, and most of the forests are lost forever.

A mango has a large single seed inside it which can grow into a new tree.

Deciduous forest

In a deciduous forest, all or most of the trees lose their leaves when summer ends. Apart from a few evergreens, such as the holly, the trees shut down for the winter. When spring arrives, there is a month before the leaves are fully out, and the sun beams through to the forest floor. So in the spring, flowers cover these forests like a carpet.

Sweet chestnut leaf

Long leaves

Sweet chestnut trees are easy to recognize. Their leaves are the longest in the forest and their bark often spirals around the trunk. You can feel the long, deep grooves in the bark.

Winter leaves

Beech leaves are very smooth and shiny on top, with a wavy edge. Young beeches, like young oaks, may keep their leaves in the winter, even though the leaves are dead and brown.

Beech leaf

White oak leaf

Jagged edge

The basic shape of most oak leaves is the same, but their edges can be different. White oak leaves are jagged. In autumn, look for acorns that have fallen from the trees.

Dormice like to hide among dead leaves.

Tulip tree

Leaf litter

Lovely litter

When leaves fall, they build up into leaf litter on the forest floor. Unlike candy wrappers, this litter will decompose (break down). Toadstools love it, and so do toads, because it gives them a damp place to hide.

Look for beetles, worms, and many other animals living in the leaf litter.

Maple forest in the United States

Of all the maples, sugar maples have the brightest autumn colors.

Blazing forest

Some forests become a blaze of red and yellow just before the leaves fall. The most colorful displays are in the United States and Canada, because of the climate and the types of trees.

The leaves of white oak trees can turn red or orange.

Coniferous forest

Most conifers are tough trees that can cope with extreme weather conditions. Their hard, needlelike leaves do not dry out as easily as broadleaves, so they do well in hot, dry climates, such as the land around the Mediterranean Sea. But they can also withstand cold icy winters – the largest coniferous forests are in Siberia and northern Canada.

Needle leaves
Pine trees are the only conifers whose leaves are truly like needles. Other conifers have leaves that are straplike or scalelike. But almost all are thick, tough, and resinous.

Female crossbills use pine needles to help build their nests.

Same smell
Hemlock trees are not poisonous. The deadly hemlock is a white-flowered roadside plant. The trees got this name because they have a similar smell.

Conifers have flexible branches so that heavy snow and ice can slide off the branch without it breaking.

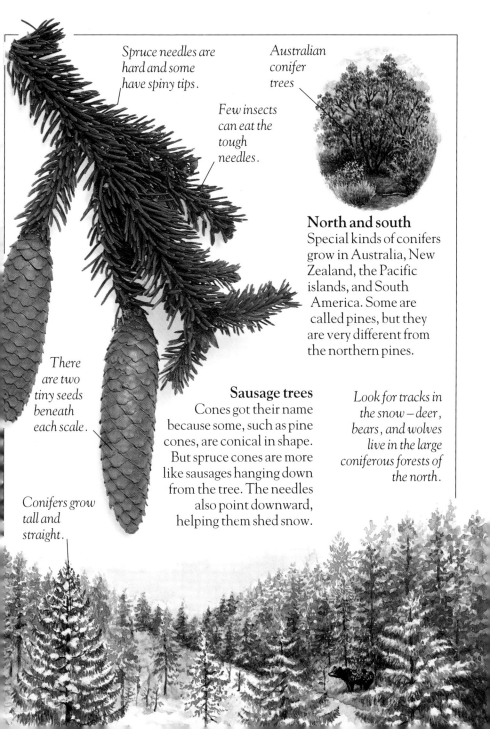

Spruce needles are hard and some have spiny tips.

Australian conifer trees

Few insects can eat the tough needles.

North and south

Special kinds of conifers grow in Australia, New Zealand, the Pacific islands, and South America. Some are called pines, but they are very different from the northern pines.

There are two tiny seeds beneath each scale.

Sausage trees

Cones got their name because some, such as pine cones, are conical in shape. But spruce cones are more like sausages hanging down from the tree. The needles also point downward, helping them shed snow.

Look for tracks in the snow – deer, bears, and wolves live in the large coniferous forests of the north.

Conifers grow tall and straight.

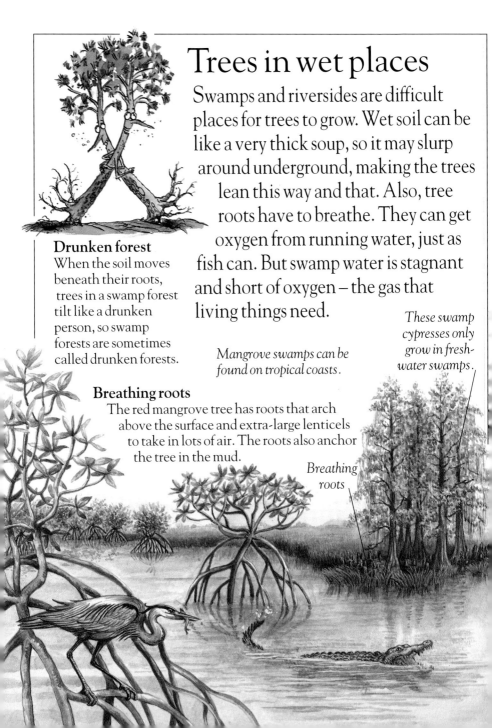

Trees in wet places

Swamps and riversides are difficult places for trees to grow. Wet soil can be like a very thick soup, so it may slurp around underground, making the trees lean this way and that. Also, tree roots have to breathe. They can get oxygen from running water, just as fish can. But swamp water is stagnant and short of oxygen – the gas that living things need.

Drunken forest
When the soil moves beneath their roots, trees in a swamp forest tilt like a drunken person, so swamp forests are sometimes called drunken forests.

Mangrove swamps can be found on tropical coasts.

These swamp cypresses only grow in fresh-water swamps.

Breathing roots
The red mangrove tree has roots that arch above the surface and extra-large lenticels to take in lots of air. The roots also anchor the tree in the mud.

Breathing roots

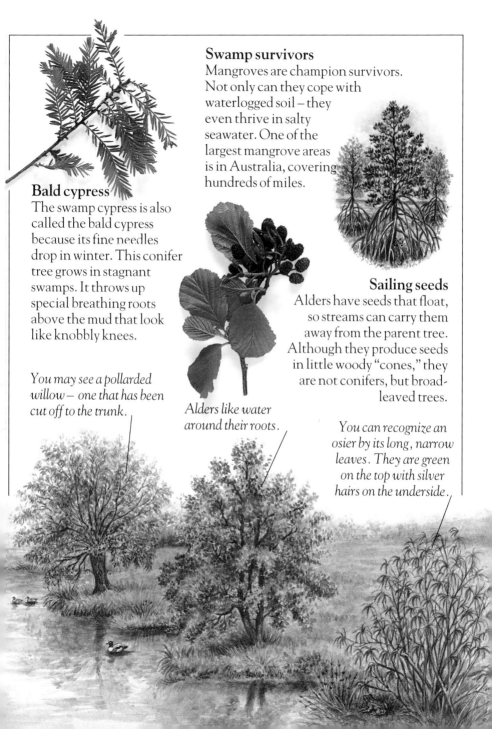

Swamp survivors

Mangroves are champion survivors.
Not only can they cope with
waterlogged soil – they
even thrive in salty
seawater. One of the
largest mangrove areas
is in Australia, covering
hundreds of miles.

Bald cypress

The swamp cypress is also
called the bald cypress
because its fine needles
drop in winter. This conifer
tree grows in stagnant
swamps. It throws up
special breathing roots
above the mud that look
like knobbly knees.

*You may see a pollarded
willow – one that has been
cut off to the trunk.*

*Alders like water
around their roots.*

Sailing seeds

Alders have seeds that float,
so streams can carry them
away from the parent tree.
Although they produce seeds
in little woody "cones," they
are not conifers, but broad-
leaved trees.

*You can recognize an
osier by its long, narrow
leaves. They are green
on the top with silver
hairs on the underside.*

Trees in dry places

Trees are very thirsty plants. The drier the climate, the fewer the trees – and the more peculiar they look. Some have bulging trunks in which to store water. All have tough, waterproof leaves. And all have special adaptations to keep away hungry animals, desperate for the food and moisture they contain.

Fight for height

In dry places, the trees are very far apart, so they don't need to compete for light. They grow tall for a different reason – to escape from leaf-eating animals. This is why giraffes have extra long necks.

Luscious leaves

The Joshua tree has fleshy leaves which are full of water. These luscious items would soon be eaten if they were not tough, sharp-tipped, and bad-tasting.

The baobab's trunk swells with water stored during the rainy season.

Giraffes like to eat acacia leaves.

Juvenile leaves

Adult leaves are long and narrow.

Up a tree

Koala bears climb up trees to reach the leaves. They are among the few animals that can eat eucalyptus leaves, which are loaded with poisons. Koalas can break these poisons down so they become harmless.

Quiver trees store water in the trunk, branches, and leaves.

Eucalyptus trees have two types of leaves – juvenile and adult.

Strong survivors

In the savannah and semi-desert parts of Africa, only a few special trees can survive. Acacias get through the dry season by dropping their leaves. Baobabs, elephant's foot trees, and quiver trees rely on water they have stored.

Look for thorny branches on elephant's foot trees.

Swollen trunk

Trees at the limits

Are you reading this in a forest? Probably not, but long ago there may have been a forest right where you are sitting now. Forests were almost everywhere until people cut them down. Although most have gone, you can still see the limits of the ancient forests – the edges where it becomes too cold, dry, or windy, for trees.

Tough at the top
Trees in high places are often shaped by wind. Look for tree sculptures on cliff tops and mountainsides.

Rowan on the rocks
The rowan is also known as the mountain ash, because it is so hardy. Some rowans grow out of cracks in the rocks. This happens when berry-eating birds drop rowan seeds in the cracks.

End of the line
When you climb a mountain, you come to the tree line. This isn't painted on the ground – it is the "line" (usually a wiggly one) made by the last row of trees.

You'll see lots of conifers growing on mountains because they don't mind the cold.

Tiny trees

The smallest trees of all, dwarf willows, grow in the Arctic. They survive the harsh climate by staying close together in a thick mass on the ground, out of the wind. If you stand next to a dwarf willow, it will only come up to your ankles.

Almost nothing grows right at the top.

Toward the peak, plants become smaller and farther apart.

Wind blown

The juniper is one of the few trees that can live in the dry Sierra Nevada mountains in the United States. Wind kills new buds – so the tree grows only on the sheltered side, making it lopsided.

Alpine meadows

Above the tree line there is scrubland (shrubs and bushes).

Trees in the garden

You may be surprised to find that the best place to see trees is not the countryside, but in towns and cities. You'll find hundreds of different kinds of trees, often from other countries, in parks and gardens. They have been planted for their colorful flowers or unusual leaves.

Handkerchief or dove?
The large white flowerheads give the pocket handkerchief tree its name. But people may also call it the dove tree.

Weeping tree
Like other "weeping" trees, this weeping ash has long, drooping branches. Weeping trees have been specially bred – so you'll only find them in parks and gardens, never in the wild.

Copper beech is the largest tree to have deep purple leaves.

The dove tree has heart-shaped leaves.

Weeping ash

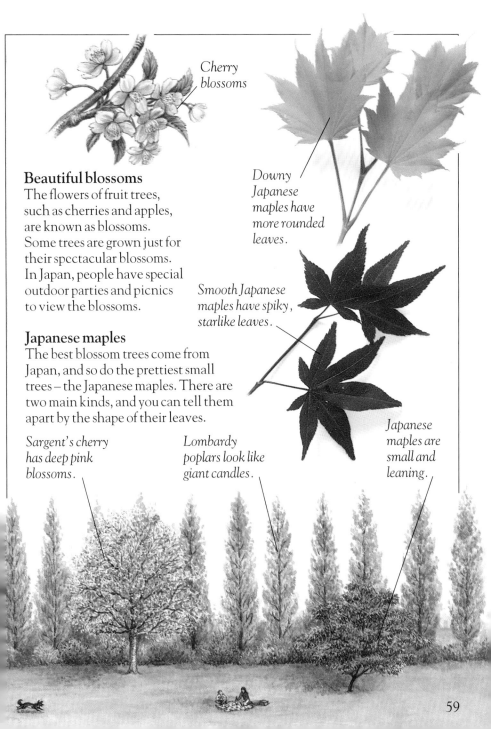

Cherry blossoms

Beautiful blossoms

The flowers of fruit trees, such as cherries and apples, are known as blossoms. Some trees are grown just for their spectacular blossoms. In Japan, people have special outdoor parties and picnics to view the blossoms.

Downy Japanese maples have more rounded leaves.

Smooth Japanese maples have spiky, starlike leaves.

Japanese maples

The best blossom trees come from Japan, and so do the prettiest small trees – the Japanese maples. There are two main kinds, and you can tell them apart by the shape of their leaves.

Sargent's cherry has deep pink blossoms.

Lombardy poplars look like giant candles.

Japanese maples are small and leaning.

Index

Acknowledgments

Dorling Kindersley would like to thank:
Sharon Grant, Chris Legee, and Wilfrid Wood for design assistance.
Ted Green for collecting tree specimens for photography.
Michele Lynch for editorial assistance and research.
Jane Parker for the index.
Royal Botanic Gardens, Kew, for supplying tropical leaves for photography.

Illustrations by:
Nick Hewetson, Tommy Swahn, Gill Tomblin.

Picture credits
t=top b=bottom
c=center l=left r=right
Frank Blackburn: 25t, 35t, 39c, 48c, 48br.
Peter Chadwick: 28tl, 28cr, 38bl.
Andy Crawford: 47.
Phillip Dowell: 30br, 43
Steve Gorton: 9c, 31tl.
Ray Moller: 41.
Kim Taylor: 34.
Matthew Ward: 20, 48.
Bruce Coleman Ltd: Jane Burton 40br; /Bob & Clara Calhoun 49c; /Eric Crichton 9tr, 10r; /John Fennell 45br; /Jeff Foott 54c; /Jennifer Fry 47cl; / Stephen Krasemann 16br; /J. Shaw 40tr; /Michael Viard 24b. L. Gamlin: 12t.
Oxford Scientific Films: / Earth Scenes/ Patti Murray 57c; /Philip Sharpe 15tr; /Tim Shepherd 36bl, 36br, 37bl, 37br.
Premaphotos: 10bl.